Camden Schools Library Service
Tel: 020 7974 6510
e: sls@camden.gov.uk
camden.gov.uk/sls

Finn and the King of Cork

For Fynn, Oscar, Sage and Olivia – MG

First published in 2008
by Wayland

Text copyright © Mick Gowar 2008
Illustration copyright © Tim Archbold 2008

Wayland
338 Euston Road
London NW1 3BH

Wayland Australia
Level 17/207 Kent Street
Sydney, NSW 2000

The rights of Mick Gowar to be identified as the Author
and Tim Archbold to be identified as the Illustrator of this Work have
been asserted by them in accordance with the Copyright, Designs and
Patents Act, 1988.

All rights reserved

Series Editor: Louise John
Editor: Katie Powell
Cover design: Paul Cherrill
Design: D.R.ink
Consultant: Shirley Bickler

A CIP catalogue record for this book is available from the British Library.

ISBN 9780750254700

Printed in China

Wayland is a division of Hachette Children's Books,
an Hachette Livre UK company

www.hachettelivre.co.uk

Finn and the King of Cork

Written by Mick Gowar
Illustrated by Tim Archbold

WAYLAND

Jim the Carter stopped his cart at the crossroads.

"Where are you going today, Finn?" he asked.

"I'm off to seek my fortune," replied Finn. "Where are you going?"
"Cork City," said Jim.

"Great!" said Finn. He climbed up and sat beside Jim. "What's in the cart?"

"Joke rubber noses and spectacles, whoopee cushions and tickling sticks," said Jim.

"All for the Mayor of Cork. The King of Cork is very unhappy and nothing will cheer him up. The queen has offered a reward to whoever can make him laugh. The mayor wants to win the reward."

They arrived at the palace at midday. Finn helped Jim to unload the boxes from the cart.

The mayor put on a rubber nose and spectacles and pulled lots of funny faces. Finn and Jim laughed like a pair of crows. "Yark! Yark! Yark!" But the king didn't even smile.

Then, the mayor sat on a whoopee cushion. Finn and Jim laughed like a pair of goats. "Tee-hee-hee-hee!" But the king didn't laugh at all.

The mayor tickled the king with his tickling stick. Then he tickled Finn and Jim. Finn and Jim laughed like a pair of donkeys. "Whooo-ha! Hoo-hoo-heee!" But the king just looked away.

"That wasn't the least bit amusing," sighed the king.

"I think you'd better go," said the queen.

The mayor, Jim and Finn bowed. But just as they were walking out of the door, the king's pet corgi dog came running up the stairs.

"I'll see if I can make the king's dog laugh," said Finn. He put on a rubber nose and spectacles. "Hullo, dog," said Finn, and he pulled a face.

The dog took one look at Finn and bit him on the ankle.

"Owww!" yelled Finn.

He fell over the dog and... Bump! Bump! Bump! Crash!

Finn rolled all the way down the stairs and into the hatstand at the bottom.

The king and queen rushed to the top of the stairs as fast as they could.

"Are you all right?" called the queen.

"I think so, Your Majesty," Finn called back.

His rubber nose and spectacles were lopsided. One of the king's fancy uniform jackets had fallen over his shoulders and the queen's best flowery summer hat had landed on top of his head.

From the top of the stairs came a gasp and a wheeze and a whoop and – a great tummy-rumbling laugh!

"Ha-ha-ha-ho-ho-ho! Yak-yak-yak!" laughed the king. "That's the funniest thing I've seen all week – all month – all year. No! That's the funniest thing I've seen in all my life! Bring that man here!"

"I'm going to give you a wonderful reward!" said the king.

"Do you have a chest full of treasure for me?" asked Finn.

"No!" said the king. "It's much better than that. You can have all of these whoopee cushions, tickling sticks and funny face spectacles. Then you'll be as happy as me for the rest of your life!"

And the king began to laugh his great tummy-rumbling laugh again. "Ho-ho! Ha-ha-ha! Tee-hee-hee! Arf-arf-arf! Yak-yak-yak!"

START READING is a series of highly enjoyable books for beginner readers. **The books have been carefully graded to match the Book Bands widely used in schools.** This enables readers to be sure they choose books that match their own reading ability.

Look out for the Band colour on the book in our Start Reading logo.

The Bands are:

- Pink Band 1
- Red Band 2
- Yellow Band 3
- Blue Band 4
- Green Band 5
- Orange Band 6
- Turquoise Band 7
- Purple Band 8
- Gold Band 9

START READING books can be read independently or shared with an adult. They promote the enjoyment of reading through satisfying stories supported by fun illustrations.

Mick Gowar has written more than 70 books for children, and likes to visit schools and libraries to give readings and lead workshops. He has also written plays and songs, and has worked with many orchestras. Mick writes his books in a shed in Cambridge.

Tim Archbold believes that making your fortune can be a difficult thing to do. Grumpy kings are hard to please, magic goats are always difficult to work with and the end of a rainbow is just over the next hill. But keep trying and have some fun on the way to your fortune...